What If?

What If We Lived on Another Planet?

Olive MacDonald

HIGH
interest
books

Children's Press®
A Division of Scholastic Inc.
New York / Toronto / London / Auckland / Sydney
Mexico City / New Delhi / Hong Kong
Danbury, Connecticut

Book Design: Michael DeLisio, Michelle Innes, and Daniel Hosek
Contributing Editor: Matthew Pitt

Photo Credits: Cover, pp. 19, 23, 30 © Pat Rawlings; Chapter pages © SpaceScapes/
Photodisc; pp. 5, 13 (bottom), 28 © NASA/Roger Ressmeyer/Corbis; pp. 6, 12, 20, 39
© Photodisc; pp. 9, 13 (top), 16, 41 © Corbis; p. 10 © Reuters New Media Inc./Corbis;
pp. 13 (middle left), 25, 25 (inset) © Roger Ressmeyer/Corbis; p. 13 (middle right), 29
© AFP/Corbis; p. 14 © NASA/Corbis; p. 33 © David Muench/Corbis; p. 35, 37 © NASA

Library of Congress Cataloging-in-Publication Data

MacDonald, Olive.
What if we lived on another planet? / by Olive MacDonald.
   p. cm. -- (What if?)
Includes bibliographical references and index.
Summary: Explores reasons why humans might want to live in space, as well as
   technical problems and scientific considerations involved in establishing a
   space colony.
  ISBN 0-516-23912-0 (lib. bdg.) -- ISBN 0-516-23479-X (pbk.)
   1. Space colonies--Juvenile literature. [1. Space colonies.] I. Title. II. What if?
   (Children's Press)

TL795.7 .M32 2002
629.44'2--dc21

2001047268

CONTENTS

INTRODUCTION

Our Earth is an incredible place to live. All of the other planets in our solar system pose serious problems in terms of supporting life. There are no plants or animals for food. There may not be any water on them. Some planets don't even have air to breathe. Others have atmospheres so poisonous they would kill a human within seconds. Some planets are boiling hot, while others are freezing cold.

Living on another planet seems impossible. Yet is it really? What if scientists figured out how to make the climate livable? Then could we do it? Are there other problems we would have to face?

Can humans cooperate with one another well enough to live together on another planet? Who would govern the new home? How would we be affected if we lived so far from Earth?

Together we will explore these and other questions. The journey into space begins right here—with ideas and plans.

Earth provides a stable home for humans that can't be matched by any other planet in the solar system.

CHAPTER ONE

Why Travel?

It's morning on the third planet from the Sun—Earth. The Sun is shining through your window, gently warming your skin. You yawn, and oxygen floods your lungs. You throw your legs off the bed and stand on solid ground. Shuffling to the bathroom, you turn on the faucet and splash cool water on your face. You consider your day: You'll eat eggs and toast for breakfast, then go to school. Afterward, maybe you'll play some video games with friends, or read a book.

This is a scene from an ordinary morning. However, you'd give it all up in a second for a chance to live on another planet. You are filled with a feeling that has always fueled the human desire to explore the stars—

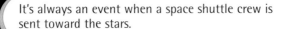
It's always an event when a space shuttle crew is sent toward the stars.

simple curiosity. In 1969, Neil Armstrong became the first person to walk on the Moon. Newscasters compared this event to Christopher Columbus arriving in the Americas. People all over the world sat wide-eyed in front of their TV sets. They didn't want to miss an instant. Why? They were excited about the new world of opportunity that was opening up.

WASTELAND

Simple curiosity could be one reason for leaving Earth to explore the stars. But what if we *had* to leave Earth? What if the air gets too polluted with car fumes and factory waste? What if there is no more clean water? What if humans ruin the environment so much that we can't grow enough food to survive? It isn't so far-fetched to think that some day we might ruin our home planet. Then we'd be forced to look for a new one.

Nuclear war is another nightmare that could make Earth uninhabitable, or impossible to live on. Soot from the nuclear explosions would block the Sun's rays. Plants would not be able to grow. Temperatures would drop and Earth would enter a new ice age. If any humans did

Earth has proven to be a sturdy home base for humanity. Yet the destruction caused by a nuclear explosion could make parts of our planet unlivable.

survive, they would be living in a world of poisoned air and water. People might be forced to live out their days and nights underground.

When nuclear bombs were dropped on the Japanese cities Hiroshima and Nagasaki during World War II, the cities were destroyed. The environment became toxic, or poisonous. Even years after the bombings, babies were being born with serious illnesses caused by the effects of nuclear radiation.

Space Hop

There might also be fun reasons to travel to another planet. In April 2001, American Dennis Tito spent twenty million dollars for a six-day trip to the International Space Station (ISS). The ISS is a floating habitat in space. It may become the first permanent space colony. Once completed, it will be the largest space station ever built. It will be about the length of a football field, with a mass of one million pounds (450,000 kilograms). The first components, or pieces, were carted into space in 1998. It may not be completed until 2006. Delivering all of the ISS components into space will take forty-four flights.

Billionaire Dennis Tito became the first person to pay for a journey into space. At twenty million dollars, it was some expensive ride!

Routine space tourism is still a long way off. Not many people have twenty million dollars to spare. However, there is a great and growing excitement about the ISS. Many people believe it is a stepping stone toward setting up a long-term colony, or settlement, on another planet.

There is yet another purpose for setting up a space colony. It could be used as a service station for astronauts going to even more distant parts of the galaxy. Because the distances between planets are so vast, it might take astronauts years to get to their destination. Tired astronauts could refuel their spacecraft and pick up provisions, or supplies. The space colony would be like a highway rest stop. Of course, scientists have to solve many tough problems before astronauts can make trips that long.

But these are just dreams, right? Well, you might as well dream big.

DID YOU KNOW?

Salyut 1 was launched in 1971. It was constructed by scientists in the Soviet Union. Salyut 1 met with great tragedy: Its crew died during reentry to Earth.

Pioneer Space Stations

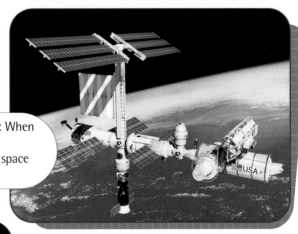

International Space Station: When completed in 2006, the ISS promises to be the greatest space station success story.

Salyut 1: The first space station, launched in 1971 (see box on page 12).

Mir: Launched by the Soviets in 1986, Mir is the largest completed space station.

Skylab: In 1973, Skylab became the first space station launched by the U.S. Skylab fell back to Earth in 1979.

CHAPTER TWO

A Trip Around the Planets

Imagine blasting off from Earth in a rocket ship bound for the Moon. After a long journey, your rocket finally sets down on the Moon's surface. You step out, take a deep breath, and choke. There is no air. You dash back to your ship to get an oxygen tank. But instead of running, you bounce. Gravity is very weak here. You can jump higher than Michael Jordan can. Well, that's a lot of fun, but you're having trouble walking from place to place.

You get the oxygen tank but now you realize you're very hot. The Sun is relentless. You're thirsty but there's no water anywhere. You head for the dark side of the

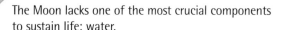

The Moon lacks one of the most crucial components to sustain life: water.

15

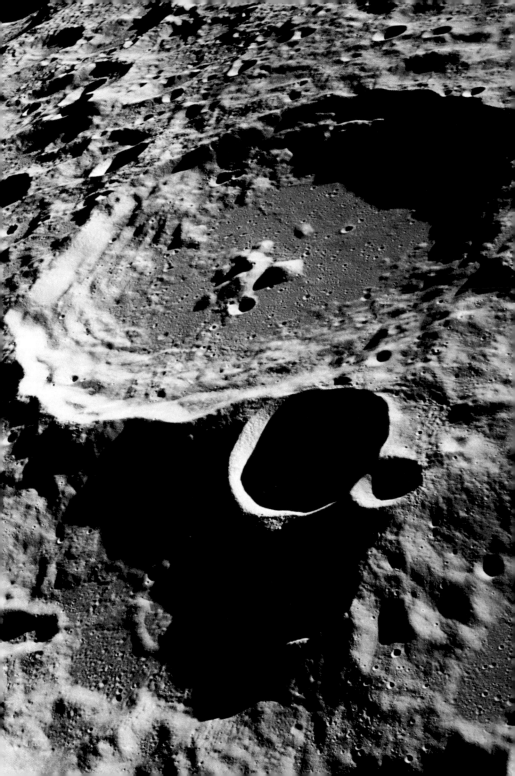

Weighty Matters

If you weigh 100 pounds (45 kg) on Earth, this is how much you'd weigh on:

Mercury: 37.8 lbs (17.1 kg)	**Venus:** 90.7 (41.1)
The Moon: 16.6 (7.5)	**Mars:** 37.7 (17.1)
Jupiter: 236.4 (107.2)	**Saturn:** 91.6 (41.5)
Uranus: 88.9 (40.3)	**Neptune:** 112.5 (51.0)
Pluto: 6.7 (3.0)	**The Sun:** 2707.2 (1225.7)

Moon to cool down. When you get there, it's bitterly cold. Earth's atmosphere, or air, retains heat at night and coolness during the day. But the Moon has no atmosphere. Depending on where you are on the Moon, it can be burning hot or freezing cold.

Now, a meteor shower begins. On Earth, most of these pieces of space debris burn up in the atmosphere as they fall toward our planet. They move quickly through molecules of air that rub against them. The friction causes heat, so the meteoroids usually burn up before reaching Earth's surface.

With no atmosphere to slow them down, meteoroids often crash onto the Moon's surface with full force.

This is not the case on the Moon. Since the Moon has no atmosphere, the meteoroids don't burn up. They hit the surface with full force, causing Moon craters. The rocks bombard the Moon, and you, like grenades.

You manage to get to your rocket ship and take off for another planet. You skip Mercury—it's too much like the Moon. You bypass Venus—there are too many earthquakes. Besides, it's far too hot—855 degrees Fahrenheit (457 degrees Celsius).

You head for Mars, where an incredible landscape awaits you. The dirt is red, because it contains large amounts of iron oxide. As iron oxide rusts, it takes on a reddish color. On Mars, there are gigantic canyons that are 4 miles deep (6.4 kilometers). That's four times deeper than the Grand Canyon. Mars is also home to the largest volcano in the solar system—340 miles high (547 km). That's sixty-eight times higher than the tallest mountain on Earth, Mount Everest.

Yet unlike Venus, Mars is bitterly frigid. It only gets as warm as 32 °F (0 °C), but it can drop to a bone-chilling -116 °F (-82 °C). The atmosphere is 95 percent carbon dioxide. That's the gas we breathe out after we have

As this painting depicts, the vast canyons of Mars are even more staggering than any we know on Earth.

inhaled oxygen. The high levels of toxic carbon dioxide would kill you. Humans would need special breathing masks. During the Martian summertime, dust storms whip across the planet's surface. As the dust blows about, the sky turns a pinkish hue. The fierce winds create craters and dunes on the planet. If we did settle on Mars, these craters and dunes might provide shelter from dust storms and meteorites.

You keep traveling to some of the outer planets of our solar system—Jupiter, Saturn, Uranus, and Neptune. But when you get there, you realize that these planets are made of layer after layer of whirling gases, such as helium and hydrogen. You cannot find any solid ground to land on.

There's only one more planet in our solar system—Pluto. It wasn't even discovered until seventy years ago. Astronomers think it was perhaps once a moon of Neptune. Then it escaped Neptune's gravitational pull. It established an orbit, or path, of its own around the Sun. No space probes have landed there yet. Our journey so far tells us that Earth seems to be the only planet that can support human life. But does that mean we should give up our dream of living on another planet? Hardly!

Forget about trying to start a colony on Saturn's surface—it isn't even solid ground!

21

Dome Homes

We know we can live in space for short visits. Astronauts have done it aboard spacecraft and on the ISS. However, no one has ever tried to live for years in outer space.

Is it really practical to try to live on another planet? Unless astronomers discover a twin of our own planet, all food, water, and oxygen would have to be shipped from Earth. And what would happen if there was an accident? The supplies might not get to you. Without food, you could live a few months. Without water, you could live a week. But you need oxygen every minute to survive.

There's another option, though—building a biosphere. A biosphere is a place where life can exist. In the 1990s, humans built a biosphere on Earth. From 1991 to 1993, eight people lived in Biosphere 2 in Arizona. It was called Biosphere 2 because the planet Earth itself is Biosphere 1. Biosphere 2 was a large bubble that held a small world within it.

In addition to humans, 3,000 species of plant and animal life were placed inside this sealed world. The different parts of the biosphere "fed" one another. They did this by providing each other with what they needed

No one knows exactly what living in a self-contained space colony would require. To test their theories, scientists built Biosphere 2, on Earth, at the end of the 20th century.

in order to live. Plants and animals in the biosphere obtained energy from the Sun. Plants created oxygen for the animals. The animal manure became fertilizer for the soil. The enriched soil made the plants grow. The biosphere was sealed so that no air or water could escape. All of the nutrients, or life-giving elements, were kept in its protective bubble.

Biosphere 2 was an experiment to see what plants, animals, and nutrients were necessary for a self-contained environment. It sounds simple. But did this great experiment run into any mishaps along the way?

The biosphere had some technical problems. Additional materials had to be brought into the biosphere after it was sealed. Also, levels of poisonous nitrous oxide rose so high that oxygen had to be pumped into the sphere.

Scientists learned that the costs of building and supplying a biosphere are high. Even after a biosphere is built, additional supplies of plants, animals, and materials might have to be sent to it. This can get expensive—fourteen thousand dollars for each pound carried into space!

Forget about money for a minute. Would it even be possible for humans to work well together so far from home?

Within Biosphere 2's bubble, eight humans worked and lived together for months on end.

CHAPTER THREE

The Human Factor

Working Together

No single government on Earth has all the knowledge and money necessary to start a colony in outer space. We would have to collaborate, or work together with, other nations. But here is where human nature can be as challenging as an inhospitable, or harsh, environment. The conflicting politics of different nations can get in the way. Would we want to share our scientific knowledge with other countries?

While working together can be difficult, it is possible. The ISS is a joint project. The United States, Russia, Japan, Brazil, Canada, and the eleven countries of the European Space Agency are building it. If we can work together

Designing and building the newest space station has become an international affair as this graphic shows.

to build a space station, we can probably build a space colony, too.

The different nations had to resolve problems in order to build the ISS. They figured out how to share power. They figured out how to share expenses fairly. The nations also decided how to share the work.

With a space colony, we would have to solve these problems all over again. We would also have to decide who would live in the colony and what language they would speak. The lesson learned by the collaboration in the ISS proves that we can work together.

■=Nations Collaborating on the ISS

Without gravity to ground them, astronauts find that moving in space can be very difficult.

Zero Gravity

Because there is no gravity in outer space, the human body can be thrown out of whack. Without gravity, you can't sit in a chair—you would float out of it. You can't eat food with a fork—the food drifts in the air. You would have to relearn the simplest activities. You would even have to rely on machines to help you breathe, eat, and sleep.

Long term space travel can take a harmful toll on the human body. Scientists believe it could weaken our body's ability to fight disease. They also believe our bone mass might break down due to changes in gravity. New research is needed to learn how we can overcome these challenges to space living.

Becoming a space colonist is a lot harder than just packing a bag and blasting off into space. A space colonist would have to go through astronaut training, just as Dennis Tito did.

Space Settlers

Let's say we did overcome these challenges and set up a colony on Mars. About thirty people live and work there. They come from a dozen different countries. Inside the colony, vegetable gardens and fruit trees grow. The space colonists raise chickens for eggs. They've brought along a huge supply of water for drinking and cleaning.

The colonists are scientists as well as pioneers. When they venture outside, they must wear space suits and gravity boots. They take samples of the soil and air. They study outer space differently than astronomers on Earth do. They send back information to Earth, helping people learn more about their universe. And just as the colonists study Mars, they are in turn studied by scientists on Earth. Scientists want to learn how the colonists' bodies and emotions adjust to life in space.

You might have success adjusting to the conditions in space. But would you be able to adjust to the other people you had to live and share space with? Imagine if all the kids in your class were cooped up together for a year or more. No one would be allowed to leave or enter. You might even get sick of your best friend if you were

The first Mars colonists would be trailblazers. Their hard work would make living on another planet easier, and safer, for future explorers.

stuck together for several years straight. Could you live with this group day in and day out?

Earth is very far from the Mars colony—286 million miles, to be exact. Scientists at the National Air and Space Administration (NASA) estimate that it would take astronauts six months to reach Mars. That means no quick rocket flights back home if you're longing for a swim in the ocean. That means you are out of luck if you want to have a basketball game with your best pal back home. And guess what? You won't see your grandparents, parents, sisters, or brothers for a long time— maybe even never again. Everything and everyone you know and love will be millions of miles away.

Sounds hard? It would be. But humans have made similar sacrifices in the past. Think of the pioneers who crossed the United States in covered wagons. Often, they didn't know anything about the land they were settling. They traveled for months in harsh conditions. Most of them never returned to their childhood homes. True, they didn't live in man-made space stations or biospheres. But their new homes probably seemed very different from the places where they grew up.

The pioneers who set out for the western United States, like astronauts, knew they were taking a huge risk by traveling so far from home.

Even if you don't have a relative who settled the West, someone in your family probably came from another country. Maybe they traveled across the ocean in a ship. They left everything and everyone they knew. They learned new skills and a new way of life. They were pioneers—just like future space colonists will be.

TransHab

Space settlers may live in more comfort than the pioneers did, though. Recently, NASA revealed a new creation—TransHab, which is short for transit habitat. TransHab is an inflatable living area. When TransHab is launched, it is folded up like a tent. Once in orbit, it is inflated with nitrogen. In just 10 minutes, TransHab swells to three times its original size! When TransHab inflates, it creates space for astronauts to live and work in. TransHab even has an exercise room with a window through which astronauts can view Earth while they work out.

TransHab may seem like a balloon, but it is much stronger. TransHab is a big improvement over old designs for living areas in space. The old designs were

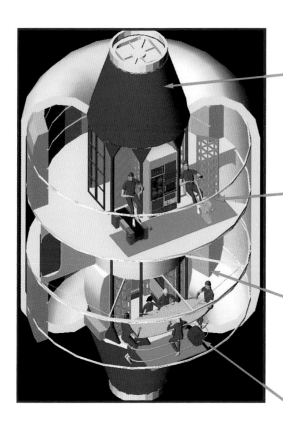

Level 4

Level 3

Level 2

Level 1

TransHab Fact Box

Weight: 29,000 lbs (13.2 metric tons)
Length: 36 ft (11 meters)
Diameter at Launch: 14 ft (4.3 m)
Diameter after Inflation: 27 ft (8.2 m)
Thickness of Protective Shell: 1 ft (0.3 m)
Level 4: Pressurized Tunnel Area
Level 3: Crew Health Care Area
Level 2: Mechanical Room and Crew Quarters
Level 1: Galley Area

made of aluminum. TransHab is cheaper to make, lighter, and safer. Its outer shell is made of a fabric called Kevlar, the material used in bulletproof vests. One expert compared TransHab's protective shell to a football. If you drive a nail into a football, it doesn't pop. Instead, a bladder system keeps the air trapped inside. TransHab is also strong enough to shield astronauts from the dangerous radiation caused by solar flares, or explosions on the Sun.

TransHab was first tested in a 6-million-gallon (22.7-million-liter) water tank in Texas. The next step is to dock TransHab on the ISS. NASA hopes to someday launch a version of TransHab toward the Moon or Mars. A TransHab trip to Mars is in the works for as soon as 2012. Once it enters orbit, TransHab will inflate and provide a floating colony for space pioneers!

The Search Is On

Our knowledge of other worlds is expanding with every space probe we launch. We have used robots to photograph our neighboring planets. These brilliant images have captured our imagination like never before. We have explored some of them with unmanned vehicles. We have

TransHab may hold the key to living in outer space. It was successfully inflated inside this giant pool of water in Texas.

analyzed their climates. We are using this new knowledge to imagine solutions to the problems of space travel.

Meanwhile, volunteers at Cornell University are cooking up a storm for NASA. They have created recipes from a set of thirty crops that may be grown in future space colonies. Someday, astronauts will follow the recipes to make their meals. The out-of-this-world menu includes scrambled tofu, lentil loaf sandwiches, and a dessert of chocolate soy candy.

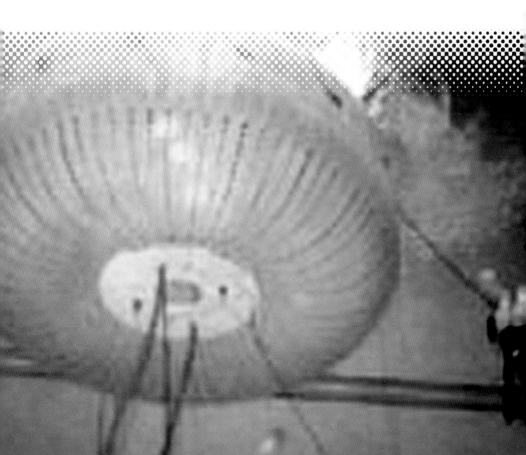

CHAPTER FOUR

Get Involved!

Take Care of Earth

While we like to dream about setting up a colony on another planet, we do not want to be forced to leave our planet. We must work to make sure the air on Earth stays pure, the water stays clean, and the soil stays rich.

Get involved with an ecology project at your school, or start one yourself. Ask students to ride their bicycles to school instead of taking a car. Start a tree-planting project. Organize a letter-writing campaign urging your senators and representatives to protect wildlife. Your favorite teacher might be a good person to talk to when you begin planning. Small efforts get results if many people work together.

The only thing that compares to the vast reaches of space is the human imagination.

Know the Sky

It's not a bad idea to learn about the planets that may someday provide our future homes. You can see the stars and even some planets simply by going outside at night. The farther you are from city lights, the more you will see. The Moon is a good object to view. You can see craters and mountains on its bluish-gray surface.

If you or your parents own a pair of binoculars, you can use them to find Venus. After the Sun and the Moon, Venus is the brightest object in the sky. The best time to look for it is dusk or dawn. It is very close to the Sun. It waxes and wanes like the Moon. Sometimes it will appear round. Other times, it will be crescent-shaped.

Stargazing Online

The Internet can take you even closer to the stars. How? On the Internet, you can view pictures from different space explorations. The Hubble Space Telescope is situated far out in space. It is more powerful than any telescope on Earth. You can access its images online.

You can also see pictures from the space probe Galileo. Galileo was launched to explore and photograph Jupiter and its many moons. Along the way, it has also taken pictures of Venus, Earth's moon, and many asteroids.

In addition, check out the photos from the space probe Ulysses and visit the Mars Pathfinder Web site. These Web sites are mentioned in the back of this book.

Read Up

As you get more serious about studying astronomy, you will want to read more about it. Some of the material may seem complicated at first. Be patient—just keep reading. The more you read, the more you will understand. The ideas will become more familiar. And one day, you may find that you've become an amateur astronomer who can share knowledge with others.

In 1997, the Cassini-Huygens mission was launched to explore Titan, one of Saturn's moons. Some scientists believe Titan may support other life forms.

NEW WORDS

amateur a hobbyist; someone who does something just for fun

astronomer a person who studies stars and planets

atmosphere the layer of gases surrounding a planet

bombard to hit with great force

collaborate to work together with others

components pieces of something

destination a place you are trying to get to

frigid extremely cold

NEW WORDS

galaxy one of many large groups of stars found throughout the universe

gravity a force that pulls things toward the center of Earth

International Space Station (ISS) a permanent base where astronauts conduct research

orbit the path of an object around a planet or the Sun

provisions supplies, such as food and water

TransHab short for transit habitat, an inflatable living area for use in space

uninhabitable not able to support life

FOR FURTHER READING

Baker, David. *Exploring Mars.* Vero Beach, FL: Rourke Enterprises, 1987.

Cole, Michael D. *Moon Base: First Colony in Space.* Berkeley Heights, NJ: Enslow Publishers, 1999.

Kettelkamp, Larry. *Living in Space.* New York: William Morrow & Co., 1993.

Rickard, Graham. *Homes in Space.* Minneapolis, MN: Lerner Publications Co., 1989.

RESOURCES

Web Sites

Hubble Site

http://hubblesite.org/

Check out a view of our solar system, courtesy of Earth's most powerful telescope. The awesome photos provided here include spiral galaxies, storms on Saturn, black holes, and the birth of a star!

SPACE.com

www.space.com

This is the ultimate Web site for amateur astronomers, featuring up-to-date news on the ISS. Check out articles about recent plans and possibilities for space tourism and colonies.

NASA

www.nasa.gov

While surfing NASA's Web site, be sure to check out links for the three sites listed below. They display some amazing images from three different deep-space explorations.

Galileo

www.jpl.nasa.gov/galileo

Ulysses

http://ulysses.jpl.nasa.gov

Mars Exploration

http://mars.jpl.nasa.gov

INDEX

INDEX

About the Author

When not writing books for young readers, Olive MacDonald raises racehorses on a ranch north of Denver, Colorado. Her interest in astronomy began when her son, Ryan, wrote a paper about the night sky for his sixth-grade class. Her entire family has loved space ever since.